Let this page inspire you to draw on the boy's T-shirt.

... and use this page for the little girl's shirt.

Decorate the bags.

You can create your own brand or store.

Design your own line of sunglasses.

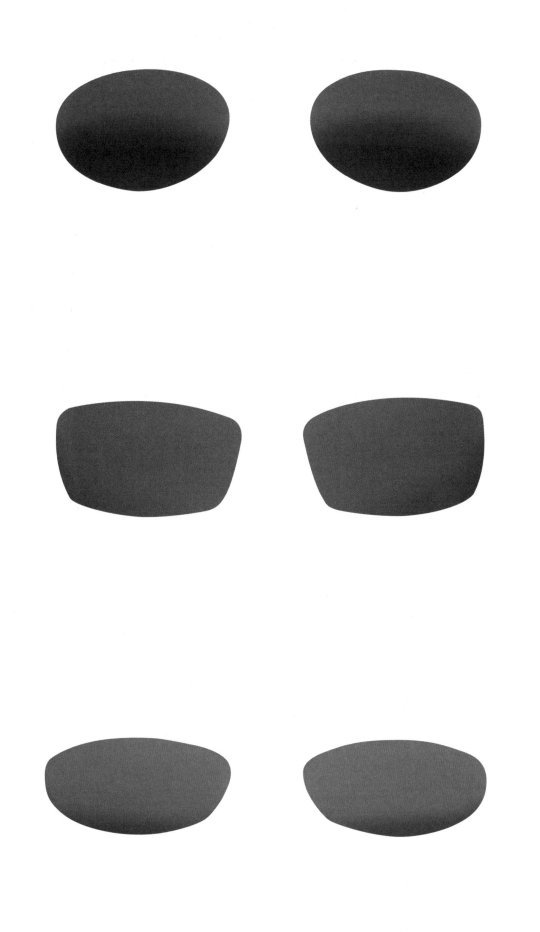

Here is a man.

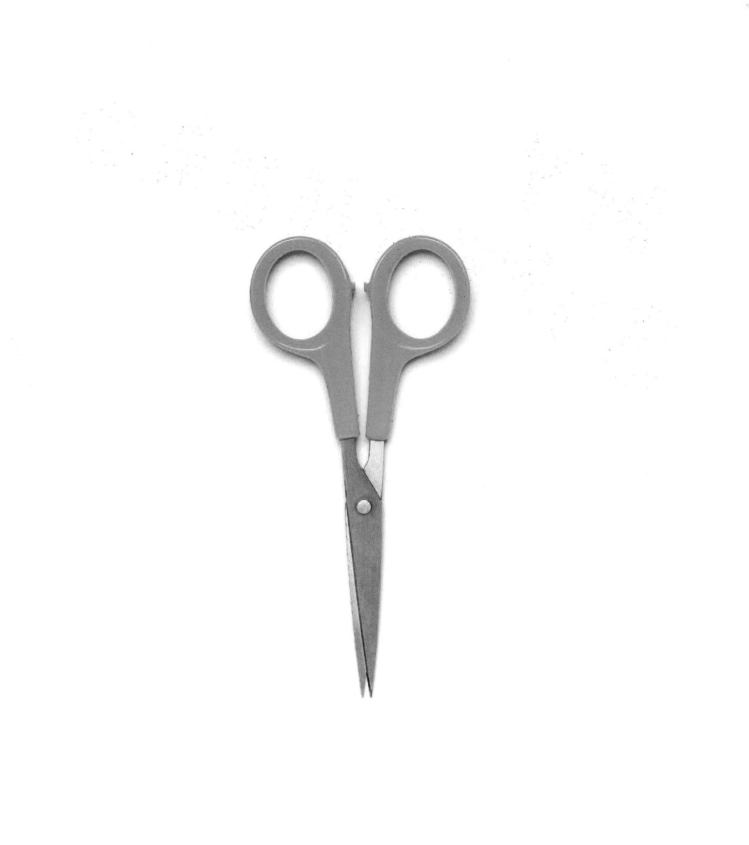

Draw a woman.

MY SUPERHERO

Here is a superhero. Give him a name and design his costume.

Plan a fashion show: for girls...

... and boys!

Complete the portraits.

Use these items to create the cover of an adventure novel.

And now, a romance novel!
Don't forget to provide a title,
the name of the author, and the publisher.

And last, design a cover for a detective novel.

Olive
Oil

Fried chicken? Steak? Dessert?
Draw what the chef prepared and also finish his kitchen.

When the masher arrives, the potatoes run away.

Fill the fruit bowl.

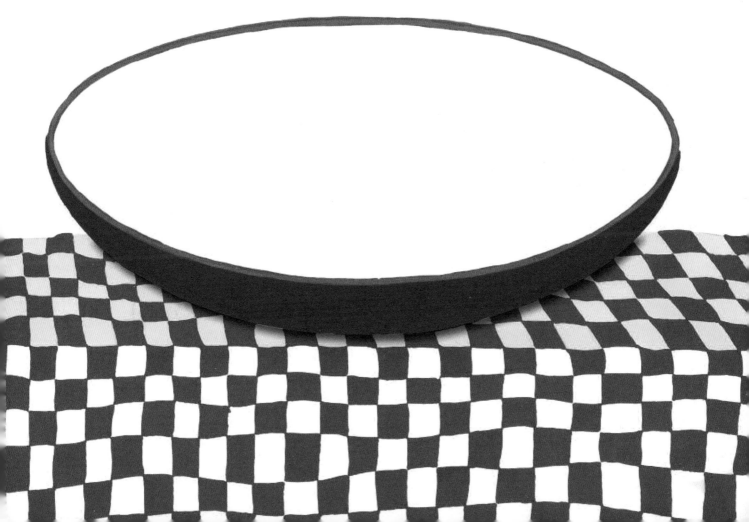

Finish the painting the artist began.

She dreams of being a historical figure.
Make it happen.

She dreams of being royalty. Help her.

What can they have on their heads?

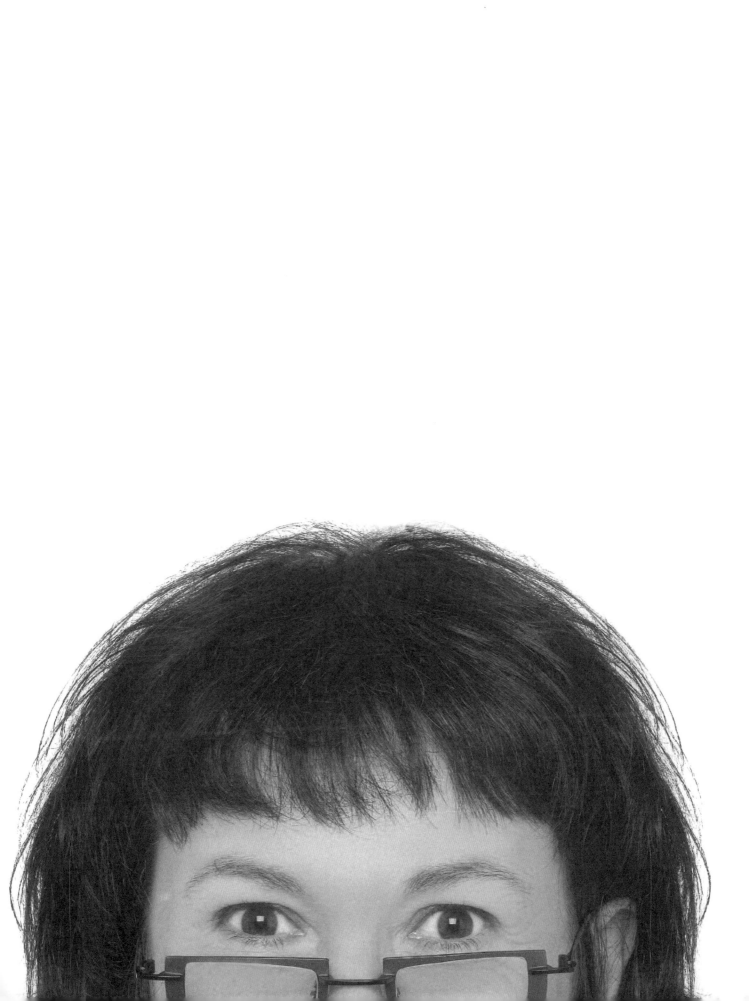

He is on the way to the summit. Draw the scene.

Finish the landscape and create some extraordinary cows.

There are dolphins and sharks in the sea. Draw them.

Make a portrait of the captain.

The florist's shop is opening. Fill all the vases with flowers.

Stems? Flowers? Finish them.

A great feast is starting.

**Finish lighting the candles
and draw the candlesticks.**

The carrot and the eggplant are getting married.

With the clothes on the following pages, dress the zucchini.

... the leek and the endive...

... the zucchini and the carrot...

... the carrot and the pepper.

Carefully cut out the clothes and accessories.

Make outfits for the guests that don't have them.

And don't forget the lemon!

A big thank you to Hippolyte and Sophia, the legs of Florence; to Arnaud and his muscled chest; to Georges and his cap, to Hervé and his brush; to Laure as Louis and Claire as a Lady; to Sabine and Fred for their expert eyes; to Tristan and his ice ax; to Bertrand and his jacket; and to Béa and her smile.
Thank you to Sam for the layout.

The cow and pirate figurines are used with the kind permission of PAPO.

There are also two paintings in this book:
Portrait de Louis XIV (1638-1715) **vers 1694, en armure devant la vue d'une ville** by Mignard Pierre (1612-1695), Mignard le Romain (dit) (atelier). © Photo RMN © Gérard Blot. You can see it at Versailles.
The Honorable Mrs Graham by Thomas Gainsborough (1727-1788) © National Gallery of Scotland, Edinburgh. The Bridgeman Art Library Nationality.

All photos are by Jean Tholance.

Pascale Estellon is the author of many books for children, including *Photo Finish* from Seven Footer Kids.

Published in France under the title *L'autre album de photos à dessiner et à colorier* © Editions des Grandes Personnes, 2010

Published by Seven Footer Kids, an imprint of Seven Footer Press,
a division of Seven Footer Entertainment LLC, NY
Manufactured in Shanghai, P.R. China in 07/10
by Stone Sapphire (HK) Limited.
10 9 8 7 6 5 4 3 2

ISBN 978-1-934734-53-7